ER
ASTROLOGY

LEO
PLAYMATE

BEATRICE E. ARQUETTE

ISBN: 1508670757
ISBN-13: 978-1508670759

Leo..
Blazing rays of Sunshine,
Oh Leo you are just too amazing,
and you know it!
King and Queen of the zodiac.
You teach that love is ecstasy,
and soon learn that love is humility!

CONTENTS

PREFACE

Hello Leo! Thank you for your courage and your sense of fun! Astrology (astra/star-logos/logic) and Eroticism (eros/desire) have been intertwined since the beginning of time. Before city lights obscured the views of the celestial quilt, women and men observed the stars and tracked their orbits across the universe. Analyzing this phenomenon for ages, tracing these planetary trajectories and corroborating over thousands of years, astrology unlocks a wealth of information; everything from the earliest concept of a calendar, the seasons and prediction of weather to the quest for who will give you the most pleasure in life and how to direct the seduction to get them.

Not only has every major culture on Earth been studying the stars, using them as a primary reference tool, every culture comes to the realization that there exist 12 human archetypes, reflected in the relative months of the year. To better describe this I have included the names of celebrities who epitomize each sign; you can compare their style to your current or future lovers. Each of these archetypes share a predisposition. Some may have a particular body structure, a unique sense of style, an emphasis on certain beliefs or a de-emphasis of others. Some are fulfilled by the pleasure of a sweet lipped kiss and some like something a bit more elaborate. Often only the aristocrats, the royal, the military and educated were allowed to use the science of astrology for love and sex. Accounts of the use of astrology to facilitate eroticism are plentiful throughout the historical record, utilized by every continent for the science of love for eons; the Chinese, Tibetans, Egyptians, Greeks, Romans,

Celtic, Aztec, Mayan and those in the West. The heavens above reflect the life on Earth; our closest example of this statement is the pull from the Moon on our tides, emotions and sex. Our Sun, a star which gives us life, acts in tandem with our Moon.

Your "Sun Sign" refers to where the Sun and constellations were located at the precise date and place of birth. Knowing your birth date, also known as the Sun sign, is a simple way to acquire hints, tricks and tips to please your current and potential lovers. As an astrologer, I know that the Moon sign and the Rising (ascendant) sign are important factors in the study of compatibility in relationships. In fact, I don't match my significant others' Sun sign; albeit, our moon and rising along with other aspects line up correctly. This guide takes the most weighted general aspects of compatibility and interprets them into simple English. The words contained here are for the curious, aficionados, professional astrological counselors and anyone who wants to really understand the sexual nature of their partner and themselves- to have extraordinary experiences over and over again. Pleasure is free and for everybody. Give and enjoy these earthly delights!

With Love,
— Beatrice

ARIES
and a Leo

Aries is ruled by Mars, the planet of sex and war. They pursue their loved ones with a dominant, burning desire and appreciate figuring out a good challenge, especially in the bedroom. This doesn't mean you will be strapped down with a gag in your mouth, but if you're interested then you can have a great night of just that. Aries is nearly as clever as the Leo in seduction, and will find the most erotic path of least resistance to get to the gold.

Leo loves giving and receiving gifts, and so do Aries. They are attracted to each other in many ways, sometimes simply the passion they both feel about life is enough to intertwine these two. They are both fire signs, and this combination can be hot stuff! The noble Lion of Leo has the broad vision that can make constructive use of the energies of Aries. As lovers, the Ram and the Lion are capable of providing each other with the ego support they both fundamentally desire. These two are both socially outgoing and both need time alone to recharge. As Fire-sign buddies, an instinctive trust already exists between you two. This is your foundation for a extremely exciting love affair.

True there are many, many similarities between these signs, but they have to be careful not to compete against each other for social standing. Always remember Aries that Leo is the King or Queen of the jungle.

Celebrity archetypes: Jennifer Garner (Aries) + Ben Affleck (Leo), Sandra Bullock (Leo) + Jesse James (Aries), Robin Wright Penn (Aries) + Sean Penn (Leo), Jennifer Schwalbach Smith (Aries) + Kevin Smith (Leo)

TAURUS
and a Leo

Strength and steadiness are key traits of the Taurus. They exude these traits with a sexy prowess and know how to use them to get what they want. Taureans are romantic and love all of the earthy delights. Give them the pleasures of food, drink, beauty and sex and they are amongst the most satisfied and loyal. This Taurus-Leo relationship sounds absolutely steamy.

Both Leo and Taurus value loyalty and commitment and these signs enjoy an outward appearance of luxury and grandiosity! They will go great lengths to get these things and could put demands on each other over material things. Taurus if you want to please your Leo, you will read "The Kama Sutra," and become a lover with imagination and style. It is an extravagance you can well afford, and Leo will be pleased that you are making a special effort. For all its airs the Leo lover can be insecure and needs confirmation of its ego to keep that positive spirit recharged. The leonine qualities of hope, confidence, and pride can be maintained with compliments and loving attention. Leo secretly wants to be your kitten, Taurus, in shining armor.

Celebrity archetypes: Delores Del Rio (Leo) + Orson Welles (Taurus), Robyn Smith (Leo) + Fred Astaire (Taurus), Debra Winger (Taurus) + Timothy Hutton (Leo), Brenda Carlin (Leo) + George Carlin (Taurus), Bianca Jagger (Taurus) + Mick Jagger (Leo), Louise Stratten (Taurus) + Peter Bogdanovich (Leo)

GEMINI
and a Leo

Your Gemini will be able to communicate and discuss almost anything at any time- it's quite a skill to behold. You may even hear of past sexual encounters that have an almost unreal quality about them, removed from what you may have ever imagined they would be willing to experience. A Gemini can be the most quick-witted of all the signs. Your conversations will be interesting and fantastic. This could be what you value most in the relationship, communication to keep things exciting. Gemini will never disappoint in the area of words.

Emotionally and sexually, Leo and Gemini slightly oppose each other as Leo is far more romantic and engaged with courtship and love. They can be fast friends, though and facile lovers. Curiosity is the motivation for experimentation with Gemini, and Leo can lead the way with ardor and excitement. Sex for Gemini is rooted in fantasy and conversation during lovemaking. Leo can provide this intellectual inspiration, with warmth, and drama.

Celebrity archetypes: John F. Kennedy (Gemini) + Jacqueline Kennedy Onassis (Leo), Megan Gale (Leo) + Andy Lee (Gemini), Angelina Jolie (Gemini) + Billy Bob Thornton (Leo)

CANCER
and a Leo

Leo is a dynamic sign that loves excitement and admiration. It can be the pussycat of your dreams, Cancer! Leos are adept in the ways of passion and feel most comfortable when they are in a state of love. While Leo is in command of the world around them and can direct it with physical action and grace, Cancer is able to navigate the social waters as well and is ultimately also interested in long term love and family..

The combination between a loving Leo and comforting and nurturing Cancer is often a delightful pairing that both understands and supports each other at all crossroads in a relationship. Cancer can understand Leos fervent need to be center stage in the relationship, and has little problem letting the Leo shine. The more you praise, the more you both will be aroused (quite possibly to insane heights of sexual abandon). Flattery will get you everywhere, but it must be sincere.

This can be an exciting, motivating and forward-moving relationship when each sign is in a more mature part of their lives. Otherwise, there can be too much confusion for the Aquarius, never really knowing which buttons to push or more directly, not push.

Celebrity archetypes: Tamara Mellon (Cancer) + Christian Slater (Leo), Jerry Hall (Cancer) + Mick Jagger (Leo), Josephine (Cancer) + Napoleon (Leo)

LEO
and a Leo

Set your controls for the heart of the Sun and fasten your seat belts in a mating of two Fixed Fire Lions! Two lions together can feel like long lost tribe members finding each other. Rough and tumble playmates, generous companions, devoted lovers. This is all possible if the egos don't get in the way. This can be quit a cacophonous romance. The romance will be the most charged it could be with these two extremely passionate Leos. But as a same Sun Sign you share each others best and also worst traits, and you will inflict them on each other either to the point of frustration or to new levels of tolerance and self-awareness.

You are mirrors for each other, and can admire each other endlessly. There will never be a dull moment between you two. Your loving will be just as loud as your fighting. Long term relationships here most often include marriage and children. Lions want to mate for life, after all. Give your heart to your Leo lover and you will receive one of equal value in return. Hearing that sexy purr is worth the effort.

Celebrity archetypes: Melanie Griffith (Leo) + Antonio Banderas (Leo), Rose Byrne (Leo) + Brendan Cowell (Leo), Sandra Bullock (Leo) + Ben Affleck (Leo)

VIRGO
and a Leo

The Virgo, pure, organized, disciplined and precise is a good influence on the Leo. Both signs have a great skill in communicating with any type of person. Virgoean emotions may be well-hidden on the surface, but inside their feelings run extremely deep and almost erotically so. Leo will be pleasantly surprised, often shocked.

When these two find each other, it often has the makings of a strong and stable long-term relationship. Both are devoted to marriage and family life and will encourage each other to be the best they can be. A Virgo is much more modest than a Leo with their talents. This can make for a nice balance. Leos are fascinated by Virgos, with their undercurrents of fantasy and sexuality that makes the leonine temperature rise. Leo is kind and generous and more tolerate of Virgos criticism, too. These traits are extremely appealing to Virgo. Leos want to protect their lover, and Virgo wants to please their partner. Leo represents mystery and hidden meanings to Virgo, and hidden sunshine. What a great gift, as life is so serious to the hypercritical Virgo. Leo may not always understand Virgo's needs for personal privacy and should not take it as a dismissive trait. If the Virgo reassures their lion that they will be back with some new tricks to teach in the bedroom and all will be well in both of your worlds.

Celebrity archetypes: Madonna (Leo) + Guy Ritchie (Virgo), Abbie Cornish (Leo) + Ryan Phillippe (Virgo), Elena Kuletskaya (Leo) + Mickey Rourke (Virgo)

LIBRA
and a Leo

There is a natural connection between Leo and Libra, that can make for a truly enjoyable love affair, and it offers the chance of a long term affair. Both signs are very romantic and need romance in their lives. Each needs a partner to feel complete, and both love being in love. Sometimes both signs will believe they are right for each other because of outside influences; be careful about that unless you like arranged marriages.

Libra and Leo tend to do a dance of giving and receiving and may compare notes as to who gets what and when. The romance there can be very methodical and disrupted by materialistic things. They are both often too calm and collected. One partner may mistake this for apathy and feel like there may be something better out there. If the two of you can only understand at all times that there is a great love under that cool Libra exterior, this relationship could work. Flattery will get you far with each other as long as it is sincere!

Celebrity archetypes: Halle Berry (Leo) + Eric Benet (Libra), Rosalynn Carter (Leo) + Jimmy Carter (Libra), Kate Winslet (Libra) + Sam Mendes (Leo), Anna Paquin (Leo) + Stephen Moyer (Libra)

SCORPIO
and a Leo

The combination of the Fixed Fire sign of Leo with the Fixed water sign of Scorpio indicates a relationship that will eventually come to a boiling point, but it may take a long time getting there. The journey may be worth it! Both signs are adept in the ways of passion and feel most comfortable when they are in lust. This pairing can be a force to be reckoned with because of the explosive combination of Leo's fiery ways and Scorpio's watery magic.

Scorpio will appreciate the way a dedicated Leo will treat them and in return give them undying loyalty. This will please the Leo even more and they will show it. A deep spiritual bond is almost a given with these two signs. If they can only focus on treating each other with the utmost respect, very little can go wrong. They both even enjoy each others' egocentric tendencies and find confidence and joy in those eccentricities.

Celebrity archetypes: Hilary Clinton (Scorpio) + Bill Clinton (Leo), Maria Shriver (Scorpio) + Arnold Schwartzenegger (Leo), Bill Gates (Scorpio) + Melinda Gates (Leo)

SAGITTARIUS
and a Leo

Sagittarians and Leos alike love adventure, fantasy and throwing themselves into love. These are very free signs. They appreciate humor and beauty, intelligence and wisdom. Sag is the lucky sign of the zodiac, and Leo believes in luck. A love affair with these two holds a promise of great gain in both emotional and practical matters. These are the golden children of the zodiac, and can be shy with each other at first.

Since Sagittarius represents Leo's Fifth House of love and romance, Leo will be naturally attracted to the Archer. Leo's eagerness will be totally charming, too, and Sagittarius will enjoy the dance. Both signs avoid drama and conflict and are considered some of the more upbeat signs in the Zodiac. They party together and understand that interaction with the public is very important to keep their energies charged and active.

The main issue would be that a Sagittarius may be less romantic and the Leo may begin to feel less appreciated. This is not the case, intrinsically, but the potential for these feelings are there. This could be a match made in heaven if these two don't get so wild that they burn each other out with their fiery ways.

Celebrity archetypes: Jennifer Lopez (Leo) + Sean Puffy Combs (Sagittarius), Bridgid Coulter (Leo) + Don Cheadle, Christine Taylor (Leo) + Ben Stiller (Sagittarius)

CAPRICORN
and a Leo

The Capricorn is determined to get what they want, and if they have gained the maturity to focus, they will definitely achieve their goals! Capricorns may be sexually cautious and become embarrassed or turned off easily, but as long as you are kind and honest, and don't mock their odd tendencies in any way, you can have an absolutely steamy time. Both Capricorn and Leo like social pleasures outside and with people. They are both concerned about their social cache and these things will play a major part in your relationship.

You can win a Capricorn or a Leo over with romance and luxury. They both appreciate luxurious gifts, although the Capricorn will act more subdued about this fact. If the Leo can understand that Capricorn only seems cold on the exterior, this could be a good relationship, both of you balancing each other out. To have a great love affair, trust and respect are two key words to remember. Capricorn expects it from others, and Leo, if attracted, will work hard to earn it.

Celebrity archetypes: Jacqueline Kennedy (Leo) + Ari Onassis (Capricorn), Iman (Leo) + David Bowie (Capricorn), Michelle Obama (Capricorn) + Barack Obama (Leo)

AQUARIUS
and a Leo

A relationship with a Leo is certain to be complex and exciting, as it is also Aquarius's complementary opposite on the Wheel of Life. Leo's Fixed Fire nature can be inspirational to the Fixed Air-intellect of the Aquarius. While Leo is in command of the world around them and can direct it with physical action and grace, the Aquarius is able to navigate the social milieu using an opposite technique.

Even though these two signs have little in common, usually, they are almost definitely attracted to one another. This could be a steamy love affair as they are both rather confident and kinky in bed.

Celebrity archetypes: Sharon Tate (Aquarius) + Roman Polanski (Leo), Whitney Houston (Leo) + Bobby Brown (Aquarius), Loni Anderson (Leo) + Burt Reynolds (Aquarius)

PISCES
and a Leo

An affair with a Leo can be a demanding relationship, but can also fulfill the needs of Pisces. It gets a strong lover in Leo, a lover that provides direction and a sense of belonging to something beyond yourself. The Mutable-Water nature of Pisces stirs the Fixed-Fire qualities of the Lion and together the affections are warmed and stimulated. Both signs are extremely passionate in almost every way. This pairing can be a force to be reckoned with because of the explosive combination of Leo's fiery ways and the deep Piscean magic. While Leo is in command of the world around them and can direct it with physical action and grace, the Pisces is able to do the same thing but using a completely opposite technique!

Each sign has a lot to teach each other and each sign will listen and learn. Pisces will learn self-confidence and Leo will learn to think more of others' first and foremost. As long as fiery Leo doesn't emotionally burn the Pisces and as long as watery Pisces doesn't squash Leo's ambition- this will be a very exciting coupling.

Celebrity archetypes: Lucille Ball (Leo) + Desi Arnaz (Pisces), Bernadette Peters (Pisces) + Steve Martin (Leo), Tea Leoni (Pisces) + David Duchovny (Leo)

Leo..
Blazing rays of Sunshine,
Oh Leo you are just too amazing,
and you know it!
King and Queen of the zodiac.
You teach that love is ecstasy,
and soon learn that love is humility!

Made in the USA
Monee, IL
10 August 2022